Brooklyn Biker
AND OTHER POEMS

memories of a street poet

by Burton Rosenburgh

© Copyright 2000 by Burton Rosenburgh

All rights reserved. No part of this book may be reproduced, stored in any retrieval system, or transmitted in any form or by any means, electronic, mechanical, photocopying, recording, or otherwise, without the prior written permission of the copyright owner, except in the case of quotations embodied in critical articles and reviews.

For information regarding this publication, or additional copies, please contact your local book store, or MHR Designs, Inc.

FIRST EDITION

Library of Congress Control Number: 00-092836

ISBN number: 0-9706276-0-2

Printed in the United States of America

Rear cover photo by Marti Rosenburgh

Published 2000 by: MHR Designs, Inc.
7844 Travelers Tree Drive
Boca Raton, Florida 33433
(561) 361-9800
Fax (561) 361-8350
E-mail: bklynbikerpoems@cs.com

Printed by Fine Printing Impressions, Boca Raton, Florida 33432

10 9 8 7 6 5 4 3 2 1

This book is dedicated to

My Wife

Marti Hoeko Rosenburgh who picked me up when I fell and walked all the paths with me. Who taught me how to be an equal part of two. With such patience and strength she helped me learn how to love and trust...myself...then all else. She is my substance, my staff and my shield. These memories were born in the womb of her soul and belong to her for she is the true creator of this book...I am simply the chalk.

Contents

Acknowledgements   vi
Special Thanks   viii
Quotation   ix
To the Reader   x
My Poetry   xvii

Brooklyn Biker	1
The Courtyard	5
The Visit	7
Yizkor	8
Eighth Street	12
Apartment 3E	13
Street Scene	14
NYC	15
Pipe Dreams	16
Worms	18
The Palladium	20
Salute!	22
The Stairway	23
End of Story	25
Destination	26
The Walk	27
At Voyage End	28

Seedling	29
Flight 378	30
Apology	34
Platform #2	36
The Phone Call	37
Over Due	38
Camouflage	39
Timeless	41
Rock Poem #1 – Two Rocks Talking	43
Rock Poem #2 – The Storm	44
Rock Poem #3 – Low Tide	45
Rock Poem #4 – Familiarity	46
Rock Poem #5 – Perforation	47
For Maggie	48
Sunday	49
Poem for Two Voices	50
Illusion	52
Birds	54
Confession	55
Die-a-log	56
The Oarsman	58
Holiday Greeting Card	61
My Birthday Surprise	63
Home from the Hospital	65

Acknowledgements

To my son Martin – a true friend and inspiration.

To my sisters; Rosalie Arnold and Sarah Rosenburgh for their love and support.

To Dr. Paul Cooper for giving me motion and a life.

To Dr. Edward Amorosi for giving me time to write this.

To Dr. Arnold Berliner who has so kindly tended to me these many years.

To Dr. Neil Spector whose concern and friendship and care helps me prevail.

To Dr. Lini Pandite – a gentle scholar, teacher, and student who takes the time to heal.

To Dr. Irl Extein who works his alchemy from the inside out and turned this rust into gold.

To Dr. Jacqueline Cape – a lone beacon in a dark starless night who saved this vessel from the rocks.

To my parents; Marty and Sophie who gave me the madness to make poetry...and the will to fight.

...And to all our wonderful friends for their kindness
...and the memories
...and the laughter.

Special Thanks

My sister Rosalie Arnold and dear friend Harvey Seslowsky who helped make this book possible; and for their dedication, loyalty, patronage and love.

Mickey Cohen for his delightful daily visits with "China" the doggie who lighted up our endless days during this long process, and for his help.

Thomas Fleury of Fine Printing Impressions for his input, hard work and great ideas.

Virginia Artrip Snyder, author and poet, for her inspiration, advice and help.

" I have an idea that some men are born out of their due place. Accident has cast them amid certain surroundings, but they have always a nostalgia for a home they know not. They are strangers in their birthplace, and the leafy lanes they have known from childhood or the populous streets in which they have played, remain but a place of passage. They may spend their whole lives aliens among their kindred and remain aloof among the only scenes they have ever known. Perhaps it is this sense of strangeness that sends men far and wide in the search for something permanent, to which they may attach themselves. Perhaps some deep-rooted atavism urges the wanderer back to lands which his ancestors left in the dim beginnings of history. Sometimes a man hits upon a place to which he mysteriously feels that he belongs. Here is the home he sought, and he will settle amid scenes that he has never seen before, among men he has never known, as though they were familiar to him from his birth. Here at last he finds rest. " -
W. Somerset Maughan - (from The Moon and Sixpence - 1919)

To the Reader

I was born September 17, 1938 in New York City when the world was in turmoil and America was in puberty.

I grew up on the teaming immigrant streets of The Lower East Side amongst pushcarts and secret alleys and temples of all denominations in tenements that smelled of soup. I can still see the smoke rising from the burning effigies of the Japanese and Germans hanging from the light poles as I walked home from school.

My parents were immigrants – uneducated victims of the pograms of Europe and the depression here. They carried their frustration and anger and humility like spears. I can still feel the anger.

My father would use part of his meager salary to bathe us in the wonders and mysteries of the great city – The Circus at Madison Square Garden, Radio City Music Hall, Yankee Stadium, Ebbet's Field, The Double-Decker Fifth Avenue Bus where I peered through the trees lining Central Park up to marble penthouses, Little Italy, rooftops, ice cream on fire escapes in the summer, sledding in Central Park, The Museum of Natural History where I would wander the plains of Africa, The Planetarium where I would roam the universe, political rallies, the restaurant in the back of the bakery, Chinatown, the pickle man, Mama Leone's, the cavernous markets of Essex Street, block parties, egg-creams, Yiddish Theater, Coney Island – I can still taste the hot dogs.

My father was a local movie theater manager in small neighborhoods where he would also produce vaudeville shows and events. It was the age before television when the local movie house was the center of community life. As a youngster I would huddle in the shadows backstage and pull the curtains for the films and events, and help the stagehands with the lights. It was time for Movie-Tone News and Bugs Bunny and Busby Berkeley and Abbot and Costello and Errol Flynn and Tyrone Power and Frank Capra and Fred Astair and Ginger Rogers and Lassie and Esther Williams and Roy Rogers and Shirley Temple and Clark Gable and Cecil B. De Mille and MGM and Judy Garland and The Wizard Of Oz. Time for dancing bears and European jugglers and strong men and magicians and local beauty contests and stars promoting their new movies...and dish night.

My father was Viennese and played the violin and listened to opera. He had great panache...and great sorrow. He bore many crosses...and many secrets to his grave.

My mother, a Russian immigrant, was highly volatile and emotionally chaotic. She played the guitar and made up little songs about feelings she only dreamed of; and cooked European-style, massive meals in great pots. In latter years she resorted to drugs and pain killers much of the time. She was a victim of the lack of knowledge of clinical depression in those days and the lack of proper drugs we have today. She died unrecognized.

When I was eleven my father lost his job. We left the bowels of the city and moved to Brooklyn which was a suburb of New York and, in part, a little like Venice and Florence and Vienna in the old days - with swarming beaches and glistening amusement parks and hard working people who rode in subway cars and lived in row-houses and grew families of children who were eager to break the bonds of mediocrity - many of whom were to become doctors and dentists and lawyers and rock and roll stars...and newspaper vendors.

I went to work when I was twelve - like my mother and father before me, and their parents before them. Delivery boy, shop work, packing trucks, waiting on tables in restaurants, working in the glittering dining rooms of the resort hotels in the Catskill Mountains - a ninety mile bus ride from New York - which was then the jewish Las Vegas.

After failed jobs and failing health my father ended up owning a deli-grocery store some ten blocks from the harbor of Sheepshead Bay. It was a small, dark shop that had to remain open sixteen hours per day, seven days a week in order to survive. My sisters and I worked around school hours with our parents to keep it going. I can still smell the herring.

I was sixteen when I left home and moved to Greenwich Village to pursue an acting career under the name of Burt Rayne. I studied with some of the masters of the time - Von Grona, Motyelov, Stella Adler, Herbert Bergdorf, Uta Hagen, John Cassavettes and Gene Frankel. I took courses at New York University in theater, writing and communications while supporting myself at odd jobs as a waiter, longshoreman and late night radio disc jockey.

I became part of the fabric of the bohemian sub-culture of the fifties - immersed in drugs, women and alcohol. Greenwich Village became my 'frat-house'. I found in the theater something I loved...and that I was good at. I thrived. I became estranged from Brooklyn and my family and entered the holy region of myself.

The fifties in 'The Vill' was a renaissance of art, theater and music. I would frequent bars and beer halls on side streets and the waterfront to see Miles Davis and Art Blakey and Thelonious Monk and Dizzy Gillespie and John Coltrane and Sonny Rollins and Ornette Coleman. It was like attending a birth.

It was the age of jazz and mambo and rock and roll and hashish and Bob Dylan and Ferlinghetti and Ginsberg and Corso and Kerouac and Camus and Acapulco Gold. Of the Circle-in-the-Square and The Actor's Playhouse and The Open Stage and The Village Gate and The Palladium, of espresso houses and after hour clubs and warm French bread and folk music and Turkish coffee and jam sessions. I can still hear the drums.

I traveled the United States with a theater group; and lived for a while in Mexico when I was twenty-one with native families up in the hills behind the hotels and stayed high and went to distant beaches amidst cliffs and jungles and monolithic rocks where 'gringos' did not go. I can still taste the tequila and hear the rocks talking.

When I was twenty-eight I married and had a son. Two years later we lost a second child to Cystic Fibrosis – an event that changed things and stayed with us forever. I can still feel the emptiness.

We moved from place to place trying to better ourselves. I tried to continue my acting career while supporting us waiting on tables – a situation that neither sat well with my father's ghost or my wife's parents. I eventually abandoned all artistic pursuits...I lost the magic. I went out and bought a fifty dollar blue suit at Klein's, a tie at Tie City, a pair of black Thom McAn shoes, and a white shirt at H. L. Green. Every morning I bought The New York Times, sat in a coffee shop and went through the want ads. With my lack of credentials and experience in anything but theater the only positions open to me were cold canvassing and sales. So, I went to work...any job that would have me. I became an emissary of the mongers in silk shirts...a jester in a court of fools. But I wanted to be 'straight'.

I canvassed door to door, sold encyclopedias, business machines, life insurance, furniture and appliances – anything that would put food on the table...and make me feel 'worthy'...but I mostly felt like a fraud. I missed the bohemian life and the stage so I made my life a stage. I was a good actor...I played many parts, but I couldn't leave the characters on the stage at the close of the curtain so they lived to haunt me. The plays became reality.

I spent much of my time playing hooky in The Metropolitan Museum Of Art and outdoor cafés. I left job after job going back to waiting on tables for fast cash until, by accident, I found work as a traveling salesman in television program distribution for a large entertainment company called Warner Brothers – an accident which I still don't understand, but it paid well...and it was 'fancy'...and it looked good on my pride card. It was hectic and competitive work but my

Russian-Austrian-Jewish-New York-street sense of survival made me forge ahead...it became a velvet trap. I used my acting skills to seduce the buyers...and the bosses...and the women...the women. I can still smell the perfume.

I remained in the broadcasting business for the following twenty-five years with various large corporations becoming a syndicator of some renown and having a reputation as a good, tough 'street hustler' – a deal maker. I became involved in the advertising, promotion, marketing, research and management levels of the programming business. I spent most of my time in planes, rental cars, hotel rooms, restaurants and bars...bars. I can still taste the scotch.

I was earning more in a month than my father ever earned in a year...the ghosts were quiet. I had a penthouse overlooking the river in New York City and a home with a pool on two acres in East Hampton, Long Island. I paid the tuition for my son at Cornell University while helping to care for my mother. I wore a $5,000 watch, drove a $60,000 car, ate $200 lunches...and strutted...strutted; but all the while I felt like a fraud. The parts became more difficult to play...the characters were devouring me. I was still searching for validation from ghosts...and mid-life came...like a shroud.

After failed marriages and affairs I settled in to live alone. New York is a great place to get lost in. Then I met Marti...and found my soul mate...I found a certain peace...and life became a song, we traveled the world and laughed and loved...loved.

It was during 1991 that I developed a 'stiff neck' – an aching, constant discomfort which I attributed to stress and years of hauling suitcases and sample bags through airports. Although I felt a bit tired and lost some weight, I ignored these symptoms and continued working my heavy schedule and running between my two homes.

At 6:55 p.m. on Friday, February 14, 1992, during a Valentine's Day party at my home in East Hampton, I slipped on ice and fell off my front deck breaking my neck – the first two discs in my neck completely shattering. The pain was so intense it was almost holy...cleansing of all else...like nothing I ever experienced before...it made everything and everyone in my life irrelevant...nothing existed...the universe vanished...there was just the pain. I tried to stand...to wish it away...but, for the first time in my life I was not in control. We did not know if I was to live through the night...but somewhere inside me a strength beyond the ages summoned up to urge me to prevail.

My family got the most renowned doctor in the world for this particular situation who met us at New York University Hospital at 5 a.m. the following morning. During the following days of planning and preparation for what was to be an elaborate operation in an attempt to rebuild my broken neck, while my head was screwed into a devise anchored to the bed, it was also discovered that I had a large tumor in my neck which had been eating away at my spinal discs. Other doctors were brought in...other tests were performed...other conferences held...and I learned that the tumor was a Plasmacytoma caused by Multiple Myeloma (a rare and deadly bone marrow cancer) which was systemic and virulent. The prognosis was severe...I was told I had possibly fifteen to eighteen months to live; and if I did survive the operation they could not tell if I would be able to move. However, they added, it was 'lucky' that I fell so they could find the tumor and the disease...or I would have been dead in six months.

In 48 hours my entire world changed. Everything I had ever lived by, and for, and that I understood was erased...like a swipe of the blackboard. I had always been arrogant and vain...always felt immortal...always afraid of illness and death...and hospitals...and doctors – and now I was at their mercy...I was out of control...I was in the hands of the Gods.

I remember from my childhood that there was a Yiddish word in the language of the Jews – 'beshert' – which means "meant to be"...that all things were preordained...that there was a reason for everything. It was that word that I thought of that night before the operation when I laid there in the dark after the doctors and my wife left...screwed into that gizmo in the bed, tubes going into and out of my body, seeing morphine butterflies in the shadows, life measured perhaps in hours...that I thought of 'beshert'...and smiled. It was that smile that saved me. I had been a gambler and known that there were times when you got good cards and times when you ran bad cards...times when you got hot dice and times you got cold dice – but you played out the game...you tried to prevail...that there was order in all things. I smiled and all fear drained from me. I remember thinking that this was divine irony...grand retribution...that there was a message to me...somewhere. That there were reasons for me to stay...to survive...that indeed there was a grand plan in the universe and I was part of it. That all things were 'beshert'. I awoke from the surgery reborn into an exploding galaxy of pain. I can still feel the pain.

I spent the following year learning how to stand, and move, and walk with a fused upper spine. I underwent radical chemotherapy and radiation for the cancer...and, of course, was forced to retire. I put my things in order and found a renewed love for everything and everyone around me. I couldn't wait to open my eyes in the morning and greet another day. Each day became a miracle...a gift. I remember when I was a child my mother would tell an old tale about the indentation under our noses – just above our upper lip. According to the tale everyone knew all the secrets of the universe, all the knowledge was embedded in our minds...and just seconds before birth this fairy angel would come and touch our lips so that we would forget everything and be born fresh and unencumbered...and this angel left it's mark. Well, I was imbued with a knowledge...and a love for all things as I prepared to die. Everything came into focus. I knew all secrets. The mood around our house was upbeat and positive. My wife and I moved to Florida where I could die in peace and tranquility.

However, I found that I still had anger and rage and revolt in me. I became shattered by fear...by mistrust...by degradation – as cancer and it's treatments can do to one. Also going from an active, productive life to a life of somnolence and malaise, as one drug accomplished as a side effect, was deeply troubling. It was at this point that I broke down under the heavy burden of a deep depression, which haunted me my whole life and went unrecognized and untreated since the age of fourteen...now intensified by my situation and the anti-cancer drugs.

Odd thing about severe depression – you don't feel it coming on, or the silent change within yourself – you see it on the faces of the ones you care for – you hear it in their voices – you find yourself outside yourself looking in...then, if you're lucky, you make the call...and go to work...much like fighting cancer...like running a corporation...like writing a poem.

With the care and understanding of a loving wife, fine doctors, proper medications...and the will to survive – I relearned how to think...much as I had to relearn how to move...and walk. I had to learn how to love...and to trust...and to accept. I had to learn peace...and tranquility...and harmony...which is possibly what helps me to prevail...for I do begin to believe now that the ultimate cure to cancer will come from the soul and the spirit...chemotherapy of the mind. And I do prevail. But with depression, as with cancer, each day is a victory.

I often ponder my life now and wonder why I have survived this day...for what reasons have I been saved from these many mishaps...for what purpose am I here taking up this space and time? Why does this container for the soul prevail? What do these hours mean? All things are 'beshert'. Each person must find their real purpose in life in order to survive. One must have a passion...a reason to live for, or like over-ripe fruit, fall from the tree. My passion is life with my wife...and watching my son grow into a fine true man of integrity and wisdom...and to put these thoughts and reflections on paper, to finish this book.

I have kept a journal and written poetry since I was sixteen – some forty-five years ago and watched them pile up in boxes, files and folders. With the exception of holiday cards I wrote and produced for my family and friends, I have never attempted to have any of my work published or printed before, but to finish this book has become my passion...my reason to last another day. However, over the years, I have done extensive public readings met – to my delight – with great enthusiasm. As a teenager I would stand on street corners in Greenwich Village and in Washington Square Park and read to anyone who would listen. I became known as the 'street poet'. I went on to do readings both here in Florida and New York at The Chumley's Readings, The New York Literary Society, St. Marks-On-The-Bowery, The 92 Street Y Poetry Sessions, as well as many coffee-houses and libraries. My family and friends now delight at gatherings to hear me read...and urge me to publish. Possibly this is why I have survived.

The streets and roads and people and sights and sounds of my life have whispered secrets to me which I now share with you. I hope you hear them, as I do, above the din.

Burton Rosenburgh
Boca Raton
November, 1999

My Poetry

I remember in my early days at New York University – a professor, his name now long forgotten, woke me up one day by telling us what I thought was a remarkable thing that has stayed with me all my life.

It dealt with the theory of an English astronomer, who hypothesized that the universe was perfectly round – and contained everything...because, in nature, everything ultimately assumes the spherical shape – as that is nature's most perfect form. From a drop of water...to an atom...to a molecule...to a planet...to a galaxy...to a cell, etc., etc.. all things ultimately seek the spherical form. He went on to state that if the universe was indeed perfectly round – and if it did indeed contain everything – that it would be an indisputable fact that if you could stand at the very center of the universe and stare straight ahead...you would see – the back of your head. This blew my mind...and kept me up through most of his classes.

You stand before a group; whether it be your employees, or your customers, or a benefit, or a reading, or a gathering, or a celebration – and you see a crowd...that is the picture. This picture can mean many things – but you see, at a glance, one picture – a group. What brought these individuals to the point of being this group; the underlying currents of personalities, problems, questions and meanings all remain a mystery. The dynamic forces at work beyond the layers of this group lie hidden in the picture...the picture is the impression...you see the back of your head.

You drive up a scenic road and see a mountain. You see a forest – you see a gully – you see a river...that is the picture. The wildlife and bird's nests and hunters and fishermen and ancient trees with gnarled faces and hidden paths where mushrooms and forest flowers hide all illude in that picture. What timeless forces created that picture lie hidden...you see the back of your head.

A group of words – a poem – is much like a picture. The meanings and forces may lie beneath...or between...or beyond the words. It is up to you – the reader to relive the dream. To decifer the cords and tones that lie between the words...to travel the hidden paths. As with a painting a poem will have different eyes and different senses and different memories interpret the picture...as with the mountain. Poetry is morse code of the soul...postcards from beyond. With a poem you don't see the back of your head because there is no beginning nor an end. The creative forces that produce a poem are much like the faces in the crowd and the paths in the forest and the streams on the mountain and the message of a painting. They are there for you to see beyond the back of your head.

Sometimes I struggle to find a proper word, or group of words, to evoke a smell or a sound or the pattern of a heartbeat or a memory...or a dream; to put pictures in as few words as possible and, I will admit here, to illude the reader...to disguise the picture and have the meaning take shape at a second or third reading...or take on different meanings...to look beyond the back of my head.

I have tried to keep my work in the chronological order in which they were written as many of them pertain to the history of my life and feelings at the time. I started writing these poems at the age of sixteen – during my early bohemian days when I was trying to distance myself from my family and friends...and set off on my own in the Greenwich Village section of New York. As these poems go through many ages...and many stages of my life you may note changes in style and substance leading to the latter days of my life...as I changed and grew...and as I accepted my illness and battled depression...and found true love.

A word about YIZKOR. Yizkor is the Hebrew prayer for the dead. In the orthodox religion it is a custom to say this prayer twice a day – once in the morning and once in the evening over a one year period for a parent; and on certain high holidays, birthdays, special occasions and anniversaries for relatives and friends.

A word about ROCK POEMS. When I was twenty-one I lived for a while in the back country of Mexico. For a time I lived with a poor Mexican family in the hills overlooking the beautiful Bay of Acapulco. The locals were forbidden to use the easily accessible and sugar-sandy beaches of the Bay – as these were reserved for the hotel guests and tourists. So on weekends and holidays and days off from work our 'family' and other village people would take us to the distant rocky beaches of Puerto Marques, where we parked our trucks and jeeps in the forest and climbed down craggy cliffs to this magnificent paradise of a beach. Our friends would bring food and drink and guitars and drums and toys for the children and – tequila. We would spend the day until sunset – at which time the natives would take their musical instruments up into the cliffs and serenade the sinking sun as it bathed us in it's luster. At the shore of this beach stood two huge monolithic rocks which stared like centurions against the sea. I have often thought about this spot in the universe and those rocks. I have given a male and female name to those two rocks – and thus...ROCK POEMS.

The poem "BROOKLYN BIKER" is dedicated to my dear friend Mort Shuman – song writer and international entertainer – who lived for parties...and loved to laugh. We rode many paths together. He died of liver cancer in London on November 3, 1991. He was 52.

The poem "ILLUSION" was written for, and dedicated to – my wife Marti – for her fortieth birthday.

Poems

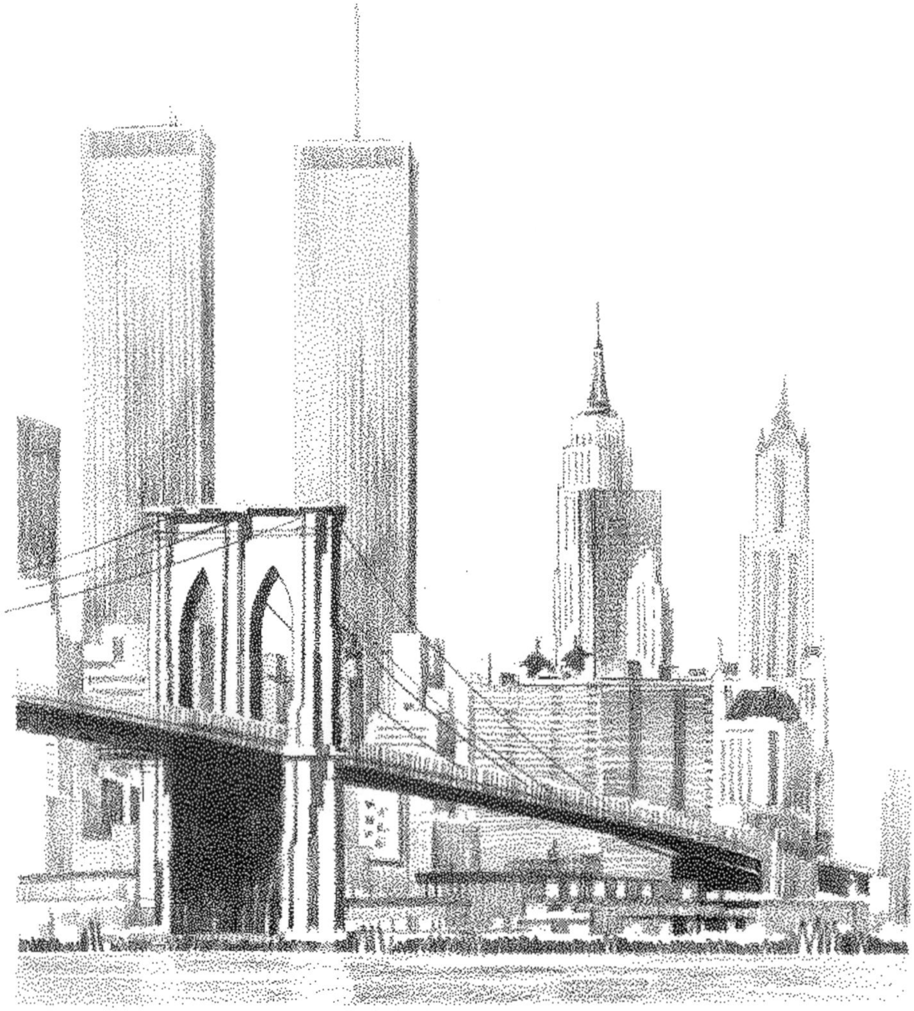

Brooklyn Biker

There was a time...
when streets
*   were long*
and rocks
*   were big...*
a sweet candy-cotton time
when fireflies in mayonnaise jars
*   lighted the way to adventure*
and popsicle sticks lasted all day.

When Morty and I
*   would touch*
the whisper-stained tires
of the banged-up trucks
*   that went everywhere*
and feel through our fingertips
the hummmmmmmmm
*   of faraway cities.*

But Morty was thirteen
and he knew the beginnings
*   and the ends of things.*
When his mother died
*   and father disappeared*
(some say the old man boarded a west-bound bus for Hell)
Morty wore his days like a broken leg.

So it was
*   on that screamy saturday morning*
that we stole bikes from a basement
*   and while we ran*
Morty whispered that we were off to...
*   Alaska!*
*   Alaska!*
*   Alaska!*

We peddled past little shacks
                       with chimneys
stainless steel seafood restaurants
                       still quiet
open-air hotdog stands
                       vats of sizzling fries
sweet upon the salty air
and grey became yellow...
yellow as we rode fast past
                       bushels of bluish clams
violet crabs with crinkly claws
past wharves and docks and fishing boats
         with white painted masts
to the mouth of the Belt Parkway
         beyond which stretched the sea
                       and dunes
and shadowed hulls of distant ships floated
         against the blues
and the behemoth distant forms of the Parachute Jump
         the Cyclone Roller Coaster
         the great Ferris Wheel
rose through the morning mist
like Pharaoh's pyramids
marking Brooklyn's land of fantasy...
                       Coney Island.
Morty turned
     and winked
     and yelled
               charge!
               charge!
and we gulped the path fast past Plum Beach.

Then it was in hushed heat
     white like fire
that we slithered down
     beneath Spring Creek Bridge
and swam...
and threw skimmers...
and spit...

and peed on piss-clams...
and rolled in the sand...
and rose from the surf wearing seaweed
  and jelly fish...
and smoked Pall Malls...
and chug-a-lugged Cocillana cough syrup...
and dreamed of places that smelled of sulphur
where fiery dragons rose in the night
  from roaring refineries
and the air felt like whiskey...
and men with tattoos sat in neon bars
  drinking beer from bottles
  chewed beef jerky
  and said – bastard!
Where rainbow-colored lights broke up the sky
  all the time
and girls laughed – with big, Juicy Fruit mouths
and smelled sweet – like the 5 & 10...
and we would Cadillac-a-dac-dac down glass avenues
honking at fancy women in high-clicking heels
  with bulging breasts and fat, sassy asses.

Where sterile young men in monogrammed shirts
  wound their Rolex souls
and looked at the world through Microsoft eyes.

Where death, like the milkman, came early
  in the morning...before you knew it
  and left it in clean white bottles.

Where we could hear the Sirens on the hill
  with their perfumed petticoats
call us out to play...
"Leave your beads home sonny"
  they would wail...
"The bookkeeping-sons-of-bitches won't hear us...
  they're too late for our song...

we want you to translate it for us – boys
in your boy-blood...
    on the walls of tombs
        before the dust gets you."

And life would be seen through
    half-opened window shades.

Then Morty murmured things I couldn't hear...
    and rolled his eyes...
    and made a noise...or two –
while grey grass claws scratched the sky...
    and gulls sang out...
    and things crawled slow upon the beach.
Morty whispered..."Go back now – kid,"
    And he went away...somewhere...forever.

Suddenly it was night...
the universe chilled...
loneliness came like a curse...
I threw secret looks at the ribbons
    of moonshine snakes in the
    waters of the Bay
and kicked cans home
where I little-boy'd-it into sleep.

The Courtyard

A fish-yellow smell
pale-yellow smell
pee
beans
green-hollow smell
oozed from ancient cracks of
*   ancient buildings*
bleaching in a horizontal sun lifting,
*   sifting with the grey heat*
from pavements sick with tar
*   and onions*
in the corners where
Giglio and I hunted
*   fire-rot*
*   deposit bottles*
*   dimes*
*   keys*
*   fireflies...*
us only thin enough to squeeze
*   through the fence*
past the man-in-a-ball who dripped
*   a brown and slimy brew.*
Twenty year old bacon fat clinging
*   to wires gone to cord*
*   black and useless.*
Paint cans – still moist with
*   that little squidge still ripe*
*   for pinching.*
Rainbow colors...
streams – long gone
walls – long gone
hubcaps shining like monuments
*   of a time long gone*
scumbags – drifting about – sterilous
*   long ago now weeds in our*
*   strangulous garden.*

*Tiptoeing – Giglio and I – afraid
        to step on rat's tails
        or rusty nails
we found a DiMaggio card
        stained with tea
and the tooth of a baby child...
Giglio smiled and put it
        on his nose,
then scratched his balls with it.
"Bang-bang-bang you're dead!"
        says Giglio – standing
        on a mattress once the fort
        of roaches
now silent in dust, snibering under Giglio,
little things with a million legs
gave life to our pasture.*

*Whoops!
Maniac Manooch with his menacing shiv
tried to scale the fence
scraping his knees spraying bloody rust
on us sparrows scrunched up in
        the cardboard box
Giglio squirting little yellow shits
        in his pants...
and we thought about dying...
"MAAA!"*

*Then...from beyond – somewhere...
        tomato sauce
        lamb chops frying in a pan
        a woman sang
        a trumpet cried
secret wishes there
in a scattered, fenced-in, barbed-wire
        speckled sun.
Paradise!
Paradise!
Paradise!*

The Visit

The old man – a passing friend from Europe
    they said –
drank my father's scotch and his nose got
    very red.
He belched and sang a song then sucked more soup
    leaving noodles in his beard.
They talked of friends – long gone –
    and relatives with diseases without names
    and the camps and the flight to Israel –
he smoked and coughed and laughed
he ripped at a piece of bread
a leathery hand pinched my cheek
    and suddenly he said
that God puts things that little boys hear
    in a suitcase inside our head
and when we were men we could unpack that case
    and use what we need
for this was the Good Lord's way of protecting
    nice little boys like me from
getting headaches from big ideas.
He spit in a rag – and scratched his ear so hard
    I thought boogers would fly from his eyes.
He smiled and patted my head and told me
    I was a good boy and would have a good life.
Well sir, that was fine I thought
    to be at last so free –
for it was then I knew exactly what I'd be –
I'd be rich and famous and travel
    to the other side of the world
I'd know a thing or two –
and no one that I loved would ever die...
but if by chance they did
they would do it in a room far off somewhere
    quiet and clean and unseen by me –
a room with no windows...
a room without doors.

Yizkor

*Late afternoons sea wind washed air
        cool enough to make you skip quick
over cracks thinking about potato pancakes
        by the stacks
to Hebrew school Hebrew school...
        Hebrew
thinking about Sara Schwartz with the pointy tits –
        Joe DiMaggio – how many hits?
But there were angels to know...
marble mountains...burning bushes...
great wars...tears of olives for the lamps...
barmitzva prayers...ancient songs to sing –
so up spitty steps – the old temple
a broken shadow against the Brooklyn sky
smelling within a musty sweet...
forgotten there in the shadows an old man
        sat between trips to the bathroom
studying his shoes or a spot upon the wall
        between trips
        between trips.
Tiptoe down the aisle of the hushed sanctuary
before the sleeping Torah in it's sacred closet
asking God to cure your father's heart...
and make you rich...
and stop your mother's bitching...
then race up secret steps to the classroom
where old green paint cracked and fell
        upon Rabbi Leshinsky – who always belched
and smelled of herring and dust – his hands
        like parched trees trembled
as they fumbled pages in the old black book
        to the prayer to learn that day.*

*Silver snakes fought around his bluish ears
a jumble of white steel-wool grew from his face –
his rhinoceros eyes blinked and teared and ran
  gooey stuff and his blue-serge belly
hung upon the desk as he bent over to read...
and the eleven of us, in a cadence harmonious
  to the Gods, murmured aloud:*

  "Yis-ga-dal v'yis-ka-dash sh'may ra-bo"

*I wondered if he wore that white yarmulke
  in the john...
there was a spot of chicken fat on his vest
the corners of his prayer shawl hung out
  from beneath his shirt
his face was a red balloon with the air rushing out
he looked like he might die any minute –*

  "B'ol-mo dee-v'ro hir u-say,
  v'yam-leeh mal-hu-say"

*Rusty radiators clunked and chinked and banged
and hissed like snakes
Stevie Klein kept coughing and sniffing and
  looking out the foggy windows
  and losing his place
Allen Kuhn swallowed his gum and gagged and
  I thought he was going to throw up
  right there –
suddenly the day was gone...
  and it got purplish out
apartments lighted up along Ocean Avenue...
I was wishing we would have meatloaf for dinner.*

  "B-ha-yay-hon uv-yo-may-hon,
  uv-ha-yay d'hol bays yis-ro-ayl"

*They brought that man back again tonight –
the one who tore his hair out when
  his wife didn't come home from the hospital –
the one who stood on the steps of the Temple
  and yelled bad things at God*

I could hear them downstairs
        getting ready for evening prayers
banging doors and rattling chairs
and all the old men hung in a web
        about the man with the bleeding head –
        and stared straight ahead – facing east
and moaned...and sang...and chewed their gums
        and bent down low to the rhythm of the ages
and they all knew the same secret
and a great wail went up –
        like the wail at Jericho
        like the wail at Mount Zion
        like the wail at Massada
        like the wall at Jerusalem
        like the wail at Warsaw
        like the wail at Auschwitz
        like the wail at Dachau...

        "**B**A-A-GO-LO U-VIZ'MAN KO-REEV, V'IM-RU O-MAYN"

And the door came down
and the walls blew apart
and a fiery thing with a flaming sword stood there
        at the gates of Eden
and we dared not look up –
we stood radiating in circular ripples
        about our father's grave where all innocence
        lay buried
sinking into the spongy spring earth
faintly aware of something drumming
like the coming of a parade – far off
        down the canyons of unseen streets.

        "Y'HAY SH'MAY RA-BO M'VO-RAH,
        L'O-LAM UL-OL-MAY OL-MA-YO"

And he went out from The Garden Of Eden
        with flames at his back
to leave a savage youth spent upon a hill –
        no...it was there yet still
upon a coach in Soho...

> *no...no.*

I remember well – yet forget that time...
> *that place when they vowed yes*
to no and stript the boy naked
and he went out into the wilderness to
> *leave this place barren of him –*
in getting from there to here
leaving now for later
to only guess at where the streams were
> *where the dreams were.*

> "Yis-bo-rah v'yish-ta-bah, v'yis-po-ar v'yis-ro man
> v'yis-na-say v'yis-ha-dar, v'yis-a-leh, v'yis-ha-lal
> sh'may d'kud-sho b'rith hu"

So he got high in Harlem with the Black Prophet
and saw a man kick death in the face
> *on a rooftop*
sucked rainbows in the Mexican hills forgetting
> *the time, forgetting the place*
and he waited for Moses to part the Red Sea
for napalm to open the roads to Da Nang
for Little Rock to hide the past in lime pits
for men in white suits to pollute the moon
and he heard – "Sayanora Hiroshima!"
or was it – "Dallas, forever Jack!"
or was it – "I have a dream!"
or was it – "Power to the people!"
or was it – "Next in line please!"
or was it – bop-bop-a-loo-mop-bop-bam-boom
> *boom!*
> *Boom!*
> *Boom!*

> "O-lay-nu vu'al kol yis-ro-ayl v'im-ru o-mayn"

Eighth Street

*Me and Bateman walking down Eighth
looking at all the fines with the
short-spike orange do-da hair
   and nose earrings
   and neon legs...
rubbing the bird...
   and short-breathing –
all the fine young things
   with beads and rings
   and tattoos and things –
rubbing the bird...
rubbing the bird...
feeling ready – rubbing the bird –
hearing inside stuff for the first time
ready to fly – more high than the sky –
quick in step to café music
   and Miles in our heads
rubbing the bird...me and Bateman –
   looking to score...
nodding at all the fines...
feeling no time to feel
looking at all the fines
with the flashy tights and purple skirts –
rubbing that old bird till it hurts.*

Apartment 3E

The computer sent along a nice
*   young man today*
crew cut and crisp khaki
a twinkle in his hazel eyes
a special smile for the day
he paid a brief respect then
*   took my phone away –*
what-a-ya-say? what-a-ya-say?

Some nice young fellow
dressed all in yellow
official helmet on his head
on a mission from Con Ed
climbed a pole and threw a switch –
my lights went out – it was as dark as pitch –
son-of-a-bitch! son-of-a-bitch!

My superintendent – his name was Pete
went down to the basement
*   and turned off my heat*
when I tell you
*   you could have hung meat –*
and I guess that's why they
*   call me – beat.*

Street Scene

Hello
sweet
sadness
of
a
window-shade
night
tell
me
your
secrets
and
show
me
the
way
to
a
hurry-up
home

NYC

*This
city
gets
you
hot
then
rapes
you
then
pulls
out
before
you
come*

Pipe Dreams

Glorious God there
  dead upon my couch
night again
  and I fall...
a death-decay perfumes the
  winds of memory

tick...

tears wake these hands to
  dream on paper
sleep screams out the window
the smoke of my hookah curls about
  stars on my ceiling
tock...

waterfalls flow where paint
  cracks were...
a neon cricket hides behind
  the shades...
Miles wears a halo hovering
  in C minor above his chiseled
  ebony brow lost in the wail
  of his horn...
my body is there upon the wall
my head floats to meet it only
  to gaze dumb with raw sockets
knowing I want not wine...
  nor food...
  nor smell of sky...
  nor touch of flesh...
  nor words...
  nor sense of pain to disturb
the vigil of my vacant head floating...
staring at my weightless body – there
  upon the wall...fall...

failing now
only the clock on my mantle is alive...
    tock...
    tick...
    tock...
    tick...
    you gone...
    they gone...
all gone tock-ticking
leaving behind God dead upon my couch
and my head floating
watching my body on the wall
fall...falling into a reverse of time
someplace beyond the pre-birth band...
a black hole sucks me in
    devours me
    plucks off my toes
    glues my feet to clouds
shattering into crystal splinters
    of blood
raining on ancient ruins...
life is a horizontal plain
time – a horizontal pain
and I – refrigerated in Hell
    will live forever – finding
    morning in a tiny, blue bottle
in a place beyond even your love...

tock...

Worms

*These eyes uncovered...bloody
this body worn
the worms are out tonight...
do I call them?
       Will they come?
A delight in hunger here
in this brain dwells cells where
       maggots feed
receding a hairline over the parched
       fragments of this skull –
the worms are out.
Do I shout lest they cannot hear?
The worms are out!
       And hunger here.*

*These eyes – worm-eaten have seen
a father draped upon a snowy pole
       to pay the rent...
a mother gone mad to catch the
       twentieth century...too late –
should I tell you buried in etcetera, etcetera –
       or let you guess?*

*Do they hesitate at my door?
Or do I hear a rubbery knock
       a slithery silence that can only
       be they?
They...they...they've taken the last note
the last word
the last drop of blood
the last lips pursed in prayer
and yet...they come –
a humming drumming beyond the wall.*

*These eyes have seen the Guru
selling sermons at Carnegie Hall,*

*the Prophet die on a roof at 93rd Street and Central Park West,
six million take gas showers clutching
       pumice soap,
the great white hope win,
MGM forget the flame throwers,
pacific fish spitting out Nagasaki,
the Silver Streak change it's last stop
       to Dallas,
somebody sit under the apple tree with
       somebody else.
They took Detroit – and are in
       all the glove compartments,
they took Xerox and hide behind
       every sheet,
IBM and left the cards in dust,
NBC and ate the tube...
they were seen in Washington, D.C.,
Times Square, Memphis, Cape Canaveral,
Kent State, UCLA, Eighth and Sixth,
Beverly Hills, Gross Point, Kings Point, Silicon Valley,
leaving Bangladesh for One Downing Street...
should I tell you more...or let you guess.*

*But now...they come – those slobbering,
       slimy, earth-damp bastards...
they come!
A silence...roaring in the ear
       can you hear?
They're up the stairs and at the door
not filled with General Foods or The AMA,
nor all chips at RCA...
they come...and come.*

*The table moves...
       it is them...
       I anoint this brain with honey.*

*Should I tell you more –
       or let you guess?*

The Palladium

Mambo!
Té Quiero!
Bailar con migo!
Andale!

Neon – spilled shimmering on
         rumbling Broadway
quite – in rusty glass-steel dreams like
         the empty shops in shadows damp
         with urine and tears.

1957 – and the city beat deep
         like the fractured factories roaring
         with Fifties glory.
Broadway beat...with a drum...far off –
         Oyay!

Mambo!

The black midget with purple zoot suit and
         long gold chain (to his ankles) taunts
         and beckons...
         invites and teases: "Howaya!"
         "Howaya folks! Step right up to paradise
         welcome to the Palladium!"

Dance up velvet steps past beaming mirrors,
         gold ropes, glass shoes
to the beat of congos and snap of bongos
Tito, Machito, Candido, La Playa.

Mambo!

Dance into the black hole of New York space.
Dance into the cave of dreams.
Dance into the never-world of sound.

The smell of Canoe and Shalimar cooks
        the sweaty air.
Breasts glisten, thighs shimmy, buttocks bounce,
legs and arms flash
        like snakes in a dance of love.

Mambo!

My hands were birds,
my feet were serpents,
my hips were churning,
I was a matador.

The purple, and blue, and black,
        and pink girls – all smiling...
all moving in opposite directions...
all wet with sweat and glisten...
all beckoning with a slither.

The music – like a needle penetrating skin...
like a spinning quartz top...
like a lightening bolt living forever...
like the birth of love.

Mambo!

Salute!

*I eat too much
drink too much
smoke too much
get high too much
screw too much...
perhaps I should have
to love someone again
or go to the mountains
or write another poem...
or light up
and have another drink
over dinner
with you...
Salute!*

The Stairway

*We struggled up the twisted landing
with the rusty cot for our first night
        in the room with the mouse.
The halls were bare and cold and rang
        with our laughter.
Our knuckles scraped – we groaned – it seems.
They watched from their car below – unbelieving –
        with a tear...I think...
we had no time to see – we were too strong
        for them...we were young...
we went on to other landings.*

*You led me up the stairs past the room
        with the fireplace and sterile glitter
        with all the games I used to play...
past the study – still locked...papers
        piled in the corners – ink dry;
past the long hall where the pictures hung
        of the us...and them all smiling
the ones we knew we didn't know
the ones who drank all the champagne
the ones who were always showing up –
        between times...but went home early
to get it done...but never did
        and stayed gone.*

*We traveled further up the landings winding
        with shadows – where I would not have
        gone – you know that...if you had not led...
yet up we went...I thought you led – I know at
        least I stumbled and you were not there
but when I turned you seemed to reach, and
        up the stair – we were gone...up again...
past his room – still sleeping – it seems forever.*

*I wanted to pause for a breath...to catch a wind,
but up we went – gliding past our joy's room
ajar with light...ha-ha-ing we went;
past the closets where the things I lost
 were humidified – and hanging...
past the room I'll get to...
past the locked room – with all my books still
 in cartons – packed tight...feeding worms.*

*Then up we went...still up – although I was afraid –
 past the bedroom...still curtains...still sheets...
still silk flowers...still memories;
but now more stairs...a turn...
 and down we went – one at a time –
not looking...not caring if we stumbled.*

End of Story

Let me recount here
the reason I loved thee –
 we had great sex.
Let me recount here
why I love thee no more –
 the sex ran out...
went from a bang to a whimper.
Suddenly we had time for other things
like realizing we were really strangers
 from the ears up.
Strangerrrrrr.

Destination

*Sometimes I look
without knowing where I'm going –
sometimes I go
without knowing where to look –
today I went where I was looking
and looked where I was going –
so...
I'll go home...
and try again tomorrow...*

The Walk

The old man and I are just kicking leaves
he doesn't see the squirrel over there
or hear the brook beyond the trees...
he kind of looks down
       studying his paces with special care
like he doesn't want to step off the world yet...
but when a robin stopped – about there
       beyond us...
he took my arm and whispered something with a
       tobacco breath mixed with damp tweed
       and wine not drank for twenty years...
he paused a bit – I think to catch his wind
       and sat tweedle-dumming on a fence
       funning at a worm with a stick
and said he'd been a lover but never loved...
a friend...but never stayed...
that he worked his whole life but forgot why
and fought in wars that weren't his...
I go on with the old man
trying to reason out the dreams with him...
wanting to tiptoe around the spaces that hurt
that make him break the buzz-silent air
       with that wet wrinkled
       I-know-I-told-you-so look...
so we go on...
we go on...

At Voyage End

*African man...African man
polished ebony
steel sinew
lion's blood and
goat's milk in your veins
hunter's eyes darting
rock-worn feet tied
in leather bonds
selling twenty dollar watches
on mad Madison Avenue
in the shadows of the billion
dollar concrete cliffs
to Ohio people...
sleeping on the floor of a
Long Island City warehouse...
where is your spear?
Which is the way back
to the grassy plains?
Oh...African man.*

Seedling

*Pretty little flower – gentle
in a faraway garden beneath
      a dewy leaf
blowing your wide awake mind
finding dreams in rainbow hues –
gold from an Acapulco sunrise
brown from an African plain
green from a Columbian jungle
red from a Panamanian mountain...
learning how to drink upside down
      on a sunny day
sleeping in the rain.
Little flower – euphoric
in a formaldehyde spring –
watching the dawn dropping acid
      on the night
the moon turning away to vomit.
Little, little flower – growing
      up in a crystal park
all your pollen being plucked
      by prophylactic stingers
over...and over...and over...
again...and again...and again...
until you cannot come – by more...
and your roots – separate and dry –
being sucked by the wise night crawlers
      until they split...
leaving you drift on a Chick Corea wind
along with sparrows escaping summer
through a silent, sulphurous night
over Coney Island and Kankakee
      to Berkley –
and the anonymity of the sea – where
      it all began –
where it ends...without a turmoil.*

Flight 378

*Tuesday
June third
6:14 P.M.
Delta flight 378
Pittsburgh, PA to Washington, D. C.
positive rate of climb
landing gear up
flaps raised
engine pressure ratio to climb
27,000 feet
72 degrees cabin temperature
4 PSI pressure*

*Hundreds of white buffaloes lounging
      in the sky everywhere.
Kaleidoscopic faces of ancient men
      with long grey beards
peering through my window observing
      me observing buffaloes
breaking into melodic cantor now
      jet rush...
whispering your name over my left shoulder
      softly...
nobody in the cabin seems to hear
      save me.*

*Tired warriors deep in fiscal sleep
carrying their baggage under IBM eyes
      or romancing martinis – there
      a scotch on the rocks –
wolves going home to nurse their meat
or off again to hunt on 378 –
my day done
telephone calls done
speeches done
reports done*

catch-up done
follow-through done
wink-smile-nod-right-on-the-one-two-three-socko
      done...
just buffaloes
and old grey ancients
and you – softly
with that first smile
      eyes lighted up – nervous
wanting hello
brow glistening in neon sweat
face framed there in mirrors and mahogany
against guitars and drums
laughter
shattering light fragments
bodies bouncing off each other
arms and legs flying
rockets off course...with you there
in the madness of The Hustle
leaving you sweaty in a silent haze
out of the smoke and bourbon perfume
turning once to see you
      slight at first...
just that smile...then the girl-woman eyes –
stopping the drums
the guitars
the laughter
time
space...
softly I shuddered back into my drink
didn't want to stop there – then
was only on my way to Xanadu...
couldn't remember the moves...
thought it was on a seventeen year old
      Brooklyn street in fall with
      the Bay over my shoulder
or Acapulco '58 in a greased starry
      tequila night left on the beach
but now...on the way to Xanadu

    it was gone –
couldn't remember
didn't care anymore
all giving was given
all saying was said
now – mute feelings numbed now
only practiced at casually
when the rehearsal was mandatory by
    crashing loneliness –
only wanting the mirrors and mahogany
and lost missiles zooming past each other
in a sweet Dewars night –
but it all stopped on that want-me smile
so I tapped the bar with my ring
said no – not again
sucked my drink –
looked away at breasts and legs
summoned up the soul creatures of the night
  to amuse me...but they would not come
  could not come...
only all of a sudden – you there over my shoulder
reaching
stretching
smiling
now laughing
now words
now eyes
a smell
a touch
something before Xanadu
before the stars...
then you...softly clinging to me in warm gulf water
touching my chest under that holy sun
putting salty kisses sweetly on my shoulders
dancing to the tide
legs wrapped together...remembering the morning
mouths finding a home in the waves...

Five thousand feet
flaps down
landing gear down
trays up
seats up
buffaloes and ancient old men gone...
coming into once gay D. C.
sparkling with domes and spires and
ribbons of highways
and music from Jason's...
ferocious friends chinking glasses
at Clyde's...
all gone...
only coming into another lonely night
without you – softly.

7:32 P.M.

Apology

I was just passing...
I didn't mean to stop
    or even say hello
you just happened to be there
    in the way
between times and I
    really had to go.
I can't even remember caring
    that you smiled
that you pressed my hand
    and said you know.
Funny...I didn't listen
but then...I didn't hear
    birds in the morning
or wind at night in the trees
or rain upon the roof
or green wood burning
or smell cinnamon...
I was sipping my life from fine crystal
    in grand halls
where power whispered
and men conquered...and won
and women with painted lips
    had the feel of velvet
and danced to bongos
and kept their promises in mirrors
and said "how nice...how nice..."
I was laughing when I saw you –
just a girl...
long of face...
there between sips –
an old and tattered book beneath your arm
    when you smiled...and caught my eye
I really meant to go.

You were just a girl
  stout of limb
with sunlight on your cheek...
and you held me
and let me weave my lies
and sip my sips...
and let me play old songs on you
while you waited tenderly for the game
  to be done...
with just the tiniest, almost invisible,
  freshly broken
tear...in the corner of your eye.
But I wore silk shirts
  and diamond rings
and stole sips in mahogany rooms
  with secret men
  bald and brittle
who told my time with gold batons...
while I bowed to their wives I bedded
  and smiled to the others
and built castles in the sand
and took morning in a teaspoon
until...
you happened by as I was passing –
just a girl...
pale of skin...
a leaf upon your hair...
and asked – "why?"
and held my ancient hand...
and touched the wrinkle on my brow...
and left a poem on my bed...
and laughed when I spilled my sips...
and loved me...with just a touch
  of tear
  in the corner
  of your eye...
before I meant to go.

Platform #2

Remember when we sat upon a dune
*   watching the sea?*
Remember when we washed sand
*   from our bodies*
and made soapy love in the shower?
Remember when we saluted gulls
*   from our balcony in our robes?*
Remember when we sprawled
*   in the Lobster Roll*
and ate fish with our hands...
joked with strangers...
*   listened to the rain?*
Remember when we searched the beach
*   for shells*
shouting dreams to the sky
planned a trip to Samarquand
and held each other in the
*   morning chill*
when you woke me with kisses?

Remember when we looked the other way
*   and didn't say goodbye at the train?*
Remember?

The Phone Call

I wanted to call you tonight
walked to the end of the room
    and back
picked it up
put it down
smoked cigarettes
sipped brandy
listened to the walls breath
listened to my skin grow
listened to my heart beat
listened to the rubber wheels
    on the wet pavement outside
listened to the laughs we had
wanted to call
    dialed
    hung it up
    dialed
    walked
    smoked
thought about calling
wanted you to know I really
    needed you
that I really learned to care
wanted us to remember together
wanted us to hurt together
    once more
wanted us to taste the tears-sweat
    once more
wanted us
    together
    once more
at 5:14 A.M. I was too weary to resist
I called
let it ring thirty-two times
you were not home
I slept
    after writing this

Over Due

*Now that it's over
must I mourn?
Expel from my soul
that one last sigh
that seems to cling
      there – hanging
to a wire hot
      to the touch
my mind swinging
swinging my mind
to the happy times...
did we cry together?
did we awake
and find sleep together?
Enough!
This stuff done damned
by once sacred things...
      and things...
this thing be best dressed
      with monuments
broken by a mist of
      silver missiles...
possibly now
that it's done
you will finally know
that I always was
      only a one.*

CAMOUFLAGE

HAIR SPRAY
ULTRA SLIM-FAST
MERCEDES-BENZ
RAP-MUSIC
THE GOLD CARD
GET-BACK-TO-ME
ROLEX
MIRRORS
A TIFFANY BOX
KEEP-IN-TOUCH
TOUPEES
SUMMER RAIN ON THE BEACH...WITH NO ONE THERE
NAIL SALONS
VINYL
CELL PHONES...IN RESTAURANTS
AU-PAIRS
I'M-SORRY
MUSTACHE WAX
PRIVATE SCHOOLS
THE CIA
LOS ANGELES...AFTER DARK
HONG KONG...BEFORE 6 A.M.
CRACK COCAINE
BREAST ENLARGEMENTS
LET'S-DO-LUNCH
VIAGRA
EMPTY FORESTS
I-DON'T-HAVE-TIME-NOW
MID-EASTERN OIL
COLLEGE FRATERNITIES

POLITICS
INSTANT COFFEE
LET-ME-KNOW-IF-THERE'S-ANYTHING-I-CAN-DO
POLITICAL RIOTS...WITH LOOTING
ATLANTIC CITY, NEW JERSEY
LAS VEGAS, NEVADA
IMPRINTED CHRISTMAS CARDS
POETRY SLAM READINGS
TATTOOS
NASA
SINGERS...WHO HAVE TO ASK PEOPLE TO CLAP ALONG
BOREDOM
PROMISCUITY
I-NEED-SPACE
YOU
ME

Timeless

It's
difficult
to
say
goodbye
when
it's
over
because
it
never
really
is

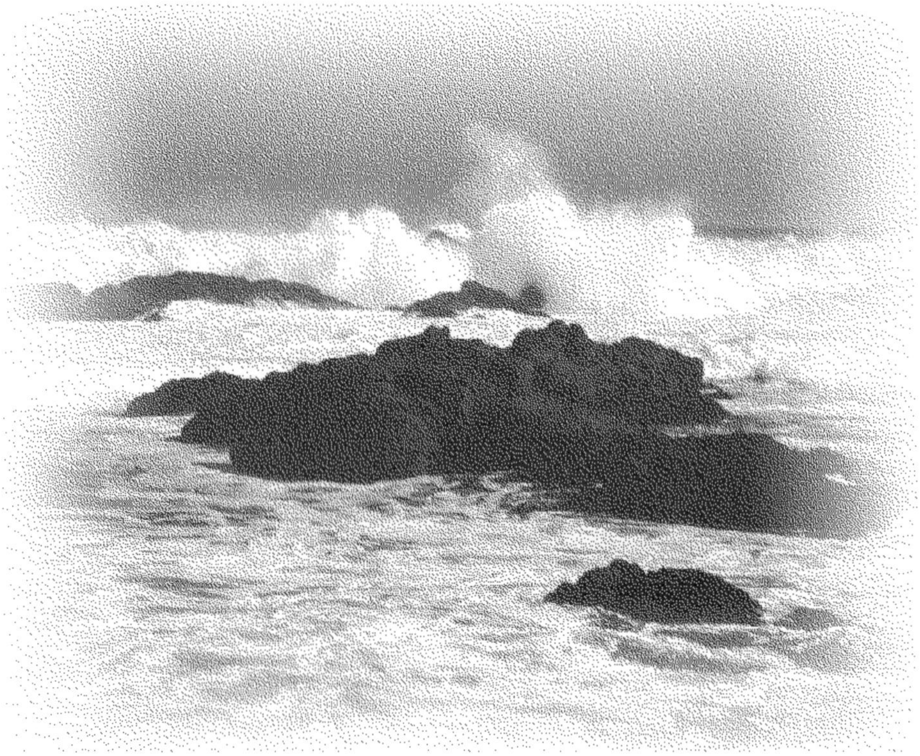

Rock Poem #1 — Two Rocks Talking

*Krankakauer and Delaportina
could not budge from that spot
they reserved in the Universe
where they could be close
       without touching –
they stood apart side by side
inhabiting the same space
       the same time
familiar – forever familiar...
each knowing the other's feelings
without feeling the other feeling...
but that particular music of the sea
       depended on them...
as you depended on me depending
you would sit there apart from me
feeling me feeling you...
without feeling me feeling.*

Rock Poem #2 — The Storm

She came...
as the night with the night
in grey chiffon languid sheets parting
then clinging around her – flowing
    she came...
lapping in desperate pleasure at
    the fringes of the sea
    moaning
biting a lip to contain a roar
slithering into ripple after ripple
    in the murky foam
rising onto...over a pale, timid shore
groping into the weeds with surgeon's
    fingers silent to disturb the
    frail passion in the straw...
softly reaching out with numbing elixir
then...spidery – drawing into a subtle hold –
warmth...deep...surrounding...penetrating...
then retreating with a cry
    in coy hesitation
but leaving a lingering dampness aglow
    with staggered lightning
coming...but not...coming from
    it's own latitude and longitude...
coming at it's own pace
    from reality...just coming...
coming...
now holding with nothing...
murmuring sounds guttural at most
    the memory of sweet pain...
trembling...stirring movement beyond
    the horizon – then still...
leaving the rocks shuddering
the air clammy to the touch...
spending the wind with a sigh.

Rock Poem # 3 — Low Tide

We remain silent at the lip
    of the sea
beyond the bells and bombs and
    grinching gears
listening to them talk of love
watching them play...
which I believe we cannot...
we are just there for them – again –
they ride the summer up our backs
we see them hold on to each other
which I assume we cannot...
the sand shifts a bit –
we draw close...then part
    in the tide...
the sky anoints us in it's blues and whites
we have to stare straight ahead beyond the reef
not needing to look for the other
we are there
    always...
we are beautiful when they come to play with us
they only appear when we are ready
we are aware of them
we are hard...and hold the sea...
we are soft...and delight the touch...
we are the last safety before the endless ocean...
they catch our foam with their lips
and slide down our backs –
but when the first smell of winter
    pearls the horizon
and stainless steel stars stab the night
from the silent sanctuary of the Universe
our tears wash out with the last tide
and they're gone...
not knowing we cared.

Rock Poem # 4 — Familiarity

I have to face you
face to face
faceless
in the silver shimmer
      of the sea –
seeing you facing me
faceless –
I can't face you faceless
but can not face
not facing that face.

Rock Poem # 5 — Perforation

The only deep thing left in me
is the hole left
by the wound you left
when you left wounded
thinking I left you wounded
when I left you leaving
thinking I would leave
before I left you thinking
about leaving a hole in me

For Maggie

There are tweedy dumps in the air
        swirling...
and purple skrills with shiny backs
        hide-and-seeking...
and neon eels with yellow tails
        flying...when you laugh.
Your mouth can catch bubbles
or eat two lollipops (grape-of-course)
or sing a Bee Gees song
        when you laugh...
your eyes roll big like moons
        and shine so far
they reflect off the hair of a leaf
        a thousand miles away
in a valley of chocolate mousse with
        peppermint flowers and
marshmallow clouds floating in a
blue-jello sky (upside down of course)...
where tree tops are covered in
        crystal laughing tears and snap
        to your smile
when you laugh

Sunday

New York Times – ink warm
herring – plate chilled
WNCN – Mozart...hmmmm
bagels – sesame seed...crisp
onion – sweet...mmmm
Face The Nation – ho-hum
a call home – uh huh
WQXR – Verdi...a ha
coffee – Italian roast
eggs – butter sizzling
nova – sliced thin
chicken soup – simmering for tonight
robes off – bodies scrubbed and talcumed
we sit amidst the plants and cats
in a sunshine shower
and listen to church bells applaud
our Sunday

Poem for Two Voices

We missed some dances at the club!

      SORRY...

We missed The Public's new play!

      SORRY...

And Andy Webber's show!

      SORRY...

We missed Trump's party!

      SORRY......DID WE MISS THE BALL?

Yes!

      SORRY...

We missed the association meeting,
open school night, Sarah's recital!

      SORRY...I SUPPOSE THE FISCAL CLOSE,
      JOE'S STOCK TIP, THE HAMPTON'S OPEN?

Yes...yes!

      SORRY...

We missed the opening of Henri's new restaurant!

      THE ART SHOW TOO?

Of course...and The San Gennaro's Fair!

       WELL...SORRY...

*We missed the subway strike, taxi strike,
garbage strike, doorman's strike. Rent
hike, food fight, tax bite!*

       THE RIP-OFF, PAYOFF, SEND-OFF?

Why yes...and Barbara Walters too!

       SORRY...

And Hillary's rally!

       SORRY...

The Jets, the Mets, the Yanks and the Knicks!

       OH YES...THE FRICK?

And the Met!

       SORRY...SORRY...

What – then?

       WE AWOKE TO BIRDS, AND CHURCH BELLS,
       HUNTED PUMPKINS, WALKED IN THE RAIN LAUGHING,
       GATHERED SEASHELLS IN THE FOAM, SANG IN
       VENICE, SPENT OUR MONEY IN FLORENCE,
       TOOK MINKY TO THE PETTING ZOO, RAN ALL
       THE WAY – NOWHERE, SLEPT LATE MONDAY,
       FOUND EACH OTHER'S SMILE...

Yes, yes...thank you.

       YOU...

Illusion

I would be a painter...that I could
trace the silver-pink slinking lines of you
upon vast stretches of virgin canvas
and follow those moist, soft curves...
while drinking a hymn to the tones
as they gush from my brushes
to blush life into thee. That I could
mix my blood with wine and add it to the oils
       to make those lips...
plunder ancient African mines for
Tanzanite dust to blend with star beams
       for those eyes...then skim moonlight
from the sea at night for that skin.

A sculptor I would be ...that I could begin
       with tool and marble
and with such tender care – softly
chisel away to the floor that
       that is not you...
but keep those breasts...breathing...
heaving to be loved...to be loosened
       from that frock...looked upon in full...
and known by lips...by fingers...trembling
       like startled doves searching to be freed.
That I could again and again and again
mold those hips...and belly and chip away
       delicately in that granite grace
to those hidden creases...then have you
       finally...forever...in a moment of
       eternal splendor...draped there
upon a pedestal in the center of my room.

*I would master physics...that a scientist
         I could be.
That I could split atoms, smash protons,
bend quarks and reduce your elements
to an essence of elixir no more than a few drops
which I could carry in this test tube in my pocket
and, while traveling my lonely steely plain,
I could drink thee...and blend thee into me...
and smell you from my nose...and feel your heart
         beat in my veins...and be one with you.
That I could claim the Universe with chalk
         and board...and roam the galaxies
         with you as pointer...and define us
in an equation that has no end.

Of music I would be...
that I could transcribe you into a melody
of a thousand violins and a harp
with an oboe here to pierce the dark.
From my podium – my hair and arms in flight
I would lead a crescendo of drums and bass
to beat as your heart in passion
and a flute to herald your smile
with chimes to awake the ripple of your smell
and a piano strong enough to mark your walk.
Then rising...like the sun...above a forest
of strings and bass – a single, haunting
French horn to sing of thee dancing nude
upon a crepuscular plain – your hair swirling
about that face – laughing...mocking the
Devil himself in sounds that only angels
make at birth.

But, alas, I'm sorry...so sorry...
for this – your poet...has only words –
the best of which are beyond my skill.*

Birds

*They appeared from the hushed white
        horizon beyond the murmurs
and fluttered around my bedside
        last night
me attached to that unseen gizmo
        with the screws in my head
getting life from a tube in my arm
        trickling from a bag beyond
my vision – for all I could see was
        a light bulb...which was my sun...
their glum-hollow eyes stare worn-weary
from searching the pathology plains
        for carrion and smelling the
        green wind for death.
I will try to stir and scare them
        a moment – or look about for weapons
        or smile at their hesitation...
but they come upon me – pecking with
        stainless steel tongues and
        glass teeth feeding on my information
        like fresh seed...
picking through maps of my bones, following
        a trail of charts through my serum...
clucking and nodding – they're gone.*

Confession

*Know that although some dreams
may not have materialized
some aspirations not met
some horizons not explored
some roads not traveled
some contests not won
some things that remain undone
that someone – some person
who has lived – truly loves you...
        for you...
for what you are
for who you are
for what you've done
for where you've been
for where you are...
truly loves you – and respects you –
        and admires you...
that you are whole in my eyes
whole in the time and space
        of eternity
and this love will live forever...
the paths we have walked are my dreams...
your smile – my pillow
your smell – my forest
your tears – my rain
I will take that – and that alone –
        with me always...
everywhere – forever...*

Die-a-log

I was cold...
  and wished I was warm.
I was warm...
  and wished I was cold.
I was hungry...
  and wished I was full.
I was full...
  and wished I was hungry.
I was frightened...
  and wished I was safe.
I was safe...
  and wished I was frightened.
I was poor...
  and wished I was rich.
I was rich...
  and wished I was poor.
I was alone...
  and wished I had company.
I had company...
  and wished I was alone.
I was without love...
  and wished I had love.
I was in love...
  and wished I was without love.
I was fierce...
  and wished I was gentle.
I was gentle...
  and wished I was fierce.

I was ignorant...
        and wished I was smart.

I was smart...
        and wished I was ignorant.

I was arrogant...
        and wished I was naïve.

I was naïve...
        and wished I was arrogant.

I am perfect now...
        and have no wishes.

The Oarsman

The oarsman struck a path
    unknown to me
through an approaching mist
    far from shore
I could already feel it's chill
which cooled my face...
not afraid I succumbed to
    his steady rhythm
tranquil thoughts like the
    waters parted silently
    leaving no wake no ripple
save my dim memories drifting in
    yesterday dreams infused
with his steady strokes which
brought a sudden smile to the
    otherwise still surface
as he cut a watery trail further
    from shore.
The oars broke the water with quiet
    respect as if they've been
    embraced there before...
his hooded back showed no effort
almost elegant in lack of motion
    he drew us farther...
I could not see his face yet thought
    I knew him...an old friend perhaps...
he rowed on and on...I forgot the
    destination yet let myself be
    taken by this silent captain
    to whatever shore awaited
    in fused sunlight beyond us...
for I could not assist nor resist
    in this journey.
We traveled on and there – beyond
    the shrubs – voices...
laughter...a gathering – a party...

I cannot see but hear the distant din
perhaps familiar voices...perhaps birds...
then a shout to me – someone to disturb
    my tranquil trip – but again
    no one there...perhaps birds.
But, it seems, I was here before
I seem to remember coming this way before –
before those striped fish streaking below
    me in dark waters...
before the buds on those trees...before
    the laughing lovers beyond the shrubs
perhaps there were dancing women beckoning
    or just trees...trees perhaps.
Faint pictures in faded frames stare
    from leaves shifting with the wind...
faces far from mind...perhaps shadows of
    this waning day.
The slipping day was drank by ancient lips
    in ancient ripples in this ancient pond...
smooth and wrinkled faces looked away...
the shore both beckoned...and refused me yet
the oarsman, oblivious to all this, continued
    his constant stroke – I thought of tapping
    his shoulder – but I could not reach.
I saw an image – vaguely familiar – in the
    mirrored surface of the water peering
intently at me...only to hide at second glance...
the reflection was older than I remember but
    the eyes were still young...the look more
    curious...perhaps cautious
like marbles from my childhood – silent
    in a box – dusty with time.

*We traveled on – the sky was an ocean streaked
        by lightning words – muffled shouts
smeared by a faint fall approaching...
it seemed our destination was at hand
for the oarsman did not take notice of such
        things but locked his gaze beyond...
whispered bird song thoughts escape this boat
        to shore and disappear in shadows of leaf
        faces I once knew somewhere but now
        begin to forget – along with day's end...
        and all else.*

*We were there – the old man rose, turned and
        gave me his hand warm to the touch...
        and we were gone...
peace came – like a slave from toil.*

Holiday Greeting Card

*It is December and I am
immersed in holidays,
shopping, partying, eating,
eating, eating, shopping – looking
at the colors of New York explode
and flash past me
into oceans of people dancing
through granite canyons bejeweled...
blazing spires scratching an icy sky.*

*The faces of children – noses
running, eyes dancing, fingers
wanting through F.A.O. Schwartz.
Sleek Modigliani women leaving
mink and chauffeurs in their wake
on mad Madison Avenue.
Ivory men huddled in smokey groups
at the Oak Bar
forgetting about sleds.*

*And your cards are coming in
daily – so nice – so different
from so many far away cities
and towns and villages
and I reflect on how fortunate
I am to know you –
to, in some way, be connected with you –
and you are all so different
like these cards, yet all
precious to me, and I think
of the seasons of my life
and the cards of my life –
the cards never sent, the
quick cards grasped at, the hip cards,
the grand planned cards,
the cards that said...
nothing.*

*And I think of how busy these
holidays are, so bewildering – never
enough time to say what we feel...
to do what we really would like to do...
to get that special person that special
little thing because the mad dashes
overtake you...kind of thing.
Yet I think now about the giving
and sharing that overtakes us, the
yearning to be connected – what this
season is really about.*

*So here it is December –
and the shopping is done.
I've plundered Bloomingdale's
and Bloomingdale's has plundered me.
The parties are dwindling – as
the notches in my belt – and all
the plans are just about finished
and I am opening your cards
and thinking of you all, whether
we glance past each other
in breath spans or
hush memories together, I
wanted to take this private moment
to wish you all, my friends,
the time, and strength, and peace,
and joy, and patience to make
all your dreams come true.*

My Birthday Surprise

*Thank you for the hushed hidden room
in the fifteenth century monastery
where we heard the monk chanting his
prayers over the shadowed twilight
hills of Orvieto...
for the passion and art of Florence
and the Leandro family – their twelfth
century apartment on the little side
street by the fountain on the square...
for the romance of Venice – the endless
hunt for the yellow glass bowl and the
adventure of the winding alley amongst
bridges and churches...
for the fury and history of Rome and the
sandwich and soda on the steps of the
Pantheon...
for the chic of Capri – the outdoor cafes
and every delicious taste of gelato...
every fragrant Mediterranean breeze...
for the peace and majesty of Positano –
sipping cocktails against God-painted
living murals bathed in church bells and
bird songs...
for the little inns with old wooden tables
laden with hams and cheeses and fruits and
breads that beckoned to our child eyes and
woke our taste for the first time...*

*thank you for the soft touch of your hand
while strolling through pastel-painted
villages and vine-covered paths; for your
glee and gusto at sharing with me the many
feasts and wines...for the fun of shopping
in a different language with different
money...for the sights and sounds and smells
that will always linger with me; and bathe
the dark times in a luster of it's own
transforming any temporary moment of pain
into a sweet memory filled with joy...
thank you for Italy...and for you.*

Home from the Hospital

My Dear's,

Our apartment, although modestly small for a New York City apartment, boasts a large fifty foot terrace facing due east with unobstructed views. Propped up here in bed on boards and pillows with my neck brace I look straight ahead and see the East River and planes circling to and from LaGuardia Airport, and endless sky and Leggo-like peaks of skyline beyond. Our terrace has become home to families of red breasted finches and brown sparrows – and it is their sweet songs against the laser-sharp streaks of red sunrise slashing through the cracks of our window blinds that woke me this morning to another miracle – another day; that and the soft warmth of sweet Marti asleep by my side, and the Minky dog snoring in the corner, and the cacophony of sounds of a waking New York – and the smells of the neighbors' coffee and eggs frying, and shampoo and cologne drift about the hallways.

These wondrous things transcend the pain and effects of the chemo and make me lie here and think of all the special moments of my life and all the things I have been so fortunate to savor; and how lucky I am to have been...and to be...what a gift this moment is...how simple joy is. I also think of all of you and how dear and special you are to me; and how much you have become part of the fabric of my life and how lucky you all have made me feel...and that I and my circumstances have touched you, and become part of your lives as well. There hasn't been a single moment during these past strange and furious weeks that I have felt alone or in need of anything. I have felt the army of you pulse through my veins and share in this battle...so there could only be victory.

There could not be a card available in any store that could appropriately express my thanks for your thoughts and kindness. Also, to my delight, there have been so many of you dear friends and family that have – each in your own way – been so special that I am afraid I am not able now to find the energy and strength to write individual notes – and so – this letter to express my deepest thanks, and those of my wife, for your overwhelming kindness...for the gestures that have been so important...the calls and cards and gifts and visits and special unexpected delightful things that you have done to make this a special time for us; for your support and friendship and caring...and for your prayers. So, like the finch's song and streaks of sunrise, you have brought us joy...thank you...and bless you.

Forever,
Burt

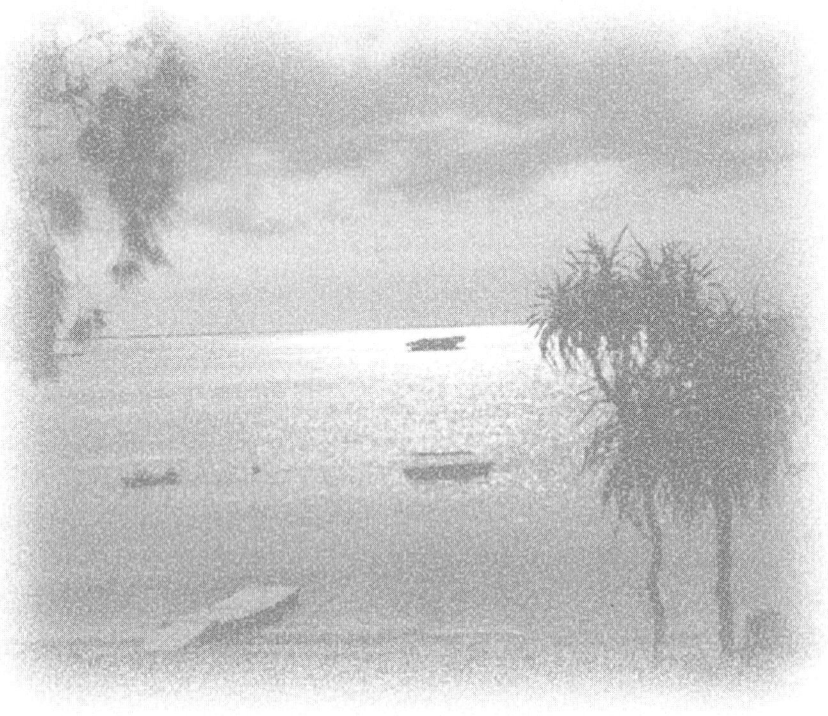